# Whispered Truth Bible Study Journal
## Trusting God's Voice, to have Victory Over Your Past

Cindy L. Smith

www.livinghopefortoday.org

# Whispered Truth Bible Study Journal,
## Trusting God's Voice, to have Victory Over Your Past

© 2020 by Cindy L. Smith

All rights reserved. No part of this book may be reproduced in any form, including written, electronic, recording, or photocopying, without written permission of the author. The exception would be in the case of brief quotations embodied in the critical articles or reviews and pages where permission is specifically granted by the author.

Although every precaution has been taken to verify the accuracy of the information contained herein, the author and publisher assume no responsibility for errors or omissions. No liability is assumed for damages that may result from the use of information contained within.

Unless otherwise indicated, Bible quotations are taken from Holy Bible, *New Living Translation,* copyright © 1996, 2004, 2015 by Tyndale House Foundation. Used by permission of Tyndale House Publishers, Inc., Carol Stream, Illinois 60188. All rights reserved.

Scriptures indicated THE PASSION are from *The Passion Translation* ®. Copyright © 2017 by BroadStreet Publishing® Group, LLC. Used by permission. All rights reserved. *thePassionTranslation.com*

Publisher Living Hope for Today
*www.livinghopefortoday.org*

Artwork: Kay Worz and Cami Bradford

Editor: Deborah A. Gaston, *www.deborahgaston.com*

ISBN 978-1-7324634-8-6

Library of Congress Cataloging-in-Publication Data

1) Fiction based on a true story 2) Abuse Prevention 2) Spirituality 3) Miracles
4) Empowerment 5) Forgiveness 6) Hope

Bible Study may also be purchased in bulk from Living Hope for Today, Cincinnati, Ohio, *www.whisperedtruth.com*

Printed in the United States of America

# Whispered Truth Bible Study Journal
## Trusting God's Voice, to have Victory Over Your Past

## Themes for 8 Week Study

| | | | |
|---|---|---|---|
| Chapters | 1-3 | Week One | *Courage* ............... 4 |
| Chapters | 4-8 | Week Two | *Faith* .................. 8 |
| Chapters | 9-12 | Week Three | *Truth* ................. 12 |
| Chapters | 13-16 | Week Four | *Forgiveness* ........... 16 |
| Chapters | 17-20 | Week Five | *Redemption* ........... 20 |
| Chapters | 21-24 | Week Six | *Obedience* ............ 24 |
| Chapters | 25-29 | Week Seven | *Trust* ................. 28 |
| Chapters | 30-34 | Week Eight | *Perseverance* .......... 32 |

## How to Use this Study

This study was written as a companion piece to the novel *Whispered Truth*, based on harrowing true events of abuse, forgiveness and hope.

The novel is used in a unique way during this eight-week study as you discover how to trust God on a deeper level in all circumstances and find healing in Him.

The *Whispered Truth* narrative and scripture are used to encourage insight into your own story. Each lesson ends with a "whispered truth" prompting you to take time to listen for God's voice. Journaling your impressions from God creates trust and allows inner healing to occur.

We can easily get stuck in the pain from past events and be paralyzed, which stops us from accomplishing God's will to have the future He wants for us. When we focus on His truth about who we are and who He is in our lives, we can be free to live the life He created us to have.

The topics that will be explored are **courage, faith, truth, forgiveness, redemption, obedience, trust,** and **perseverance.**

# *Whispered Truth*
# *Bible Study*
# *Lesson One/Chap. 1-3*

Be Strong and Courageous

**Key Verse:** *"Be strong and courageous. Don't be fearful or discouraged, because the Lord your God is with you wherever you go."* Joshua 1:9

As *Whispered Truth* opens, Denise has finally made the bold decision to leave an abusive situation. However, the voice of fear taunts her, causing her to envision the perceived dangers in following through. Fear is a response to real or perceived danger. It is a weapon in the hands of Satan that can keep us stuck in unhealthy situations. It can so immobilize us that we never fully step into God's purposes for our lives.

Describe a time in your life when the voice of fear paralyzed or immobilized you. What are you focusing on or believing if you live in fear?

_____
_____
_____
_____
_____
_____
_____
_____
_____
_____

**Read Joshua 1:1-9**

What does God command Joshua in verses 7 and 9?

_____

_____

_____

Why do you think the Lord repeated this command to Joshua? What laid in the balance if Joshua did not obey?

_____

_____

_____

Think about a situation in your life that requires courage. What lays in the balance if you listen to the voice of fear rather than the voice of God? What are the endless possibilities in God if you courageously act?

_____

_____

_____

_____

_____

Despite fear's taunts, Denise follows through with her decision to leave. Courage is defined as "the attitude of facing and dealing with anything recognized as dangerous, difficult, or painful, instead of withdrawing from it." The fear may still be present, but we don't allow it to stop us. We learn to act despite how we feel or the negative thoughts running through our minds. We trust God's truth more than our feelings. Why? Because we have a promise from God and He always keeps His promises.

**Read Isaiah 41:10 & Jeremiah 1: 6-10**

What is God's promise to you in these verses? What does that mean to you personally? How does knowing this truth help you in the face of frightening situations?

_____

_____

_____

_____

*Whispered Truth – Bible Study*

Do you trust that God's presence is enough? Why or why not?

_____

_____

_____

_____

*"One of the happiest moments in life is when you find the courage to let go of what you can't change."* Unknown

How did counseling help Denise see her past more clearly and give her courage to make different choices?

_____

_____

_____

_____

Doyle couldn't change the abuse he witnessed in his childhood. But if he wanted to change his behavior, that was influenced by his past, what role would courage play?

_____

_____

Write about something you've been able to release because you realized you couldn't change it. What effect did letting go have on you and how you relate to others?

_____

_____

_____

_____

_____

_____

_____

**Whispered Truth:** What situation are you currently facing that requires you to be strong and courageous? Maybe you need to remove yourself from a relationship or situation. Maybe you need to face your past in order to find healing. Maybe you need to have a difficult conversation with someone.

What truth is God whispering to you right now about courage? How will you apply the Word to your life?

_____
_____
_____
_____
_____
_____
_____
_____
_____
_____
_____
_____
_____
_____
_____
_____
_____

***"For God has not given us a spirit of fear, but of power and of love and of a sound mind."***
2 Timothy 1:7

# Whispered Truth
## Bible Study
### Lesson Two/Chap. 4-8

## Faith

**Key Verse:** *"God is our refuge and strength, a very present help in trouble."* Psalm 46:1

Denise is now a single working mom with grave concerns about her daughter's nightmares and acting out. If that wasn't stressful enough, she then must switch daycares because of Doyle's accusations. She starts to understand that someone is providing for her and when she meets with her pastor, he prays with her, pointing her to Jesus and she feels peace.

The definition of faith is complete trust or confidence in someone or something. Consider a time when your faith was weak or nonexistent and looking back you realized that God was taking care of you. What happened?

_____

_____

_____

_____

_____

_____

_____

_____

**Read Hebrews 11:11-12 & 17-19 Review Genesis 17:16 & 22**

Our faith is often tested when our present circumstances seem contrary from what God's word says. Sarah was 90 years old when God told her she'd conceive a son. She couldn't rely on her own efforts but only on God's ability to give her a son through her womb.

In Genesis 22, God instructs Abraham to sacrifice his son, Isaac. And yet we read that Abraham, when speaking to his servants, used the plural form of the Hebrew verb—*nashuvah* ("we will return")—rather than the singular form—*ashuvah* ("I will return"). He spoke his faith out loud by declaring 'they' would return.

Both 'faith stories' impact history, bring provision and accomplish God's will.

> Explain a test you have gone through like Abraham and Sarah and how you obeyed God by laying your will on the altar.
>
> _____
> _____
> _____
> _____
> _____
> _____
> _____
> _____
> _____
> _____
>
> Explain how that time in your life brought God's provision and peace, accomplishing His will. How did that encourage your faith?
>
> _____
> _____
> _____
> _____
> _____
> _____
> _____
> _____

The complicated maze of lies a mile long confounds Denise, but she is determined to uncover the truth. Denise calls the police to open an investigation and when the system can't tell her what has happened to Jaime, she thinks back to her childhood and God, the only one that has the answers. She has fought the negative, mocking voices in her head and started to attend church seeking to discover if God loves her for any reason at all. Faith she didn't even know she had, has given her a desire to seek God.

*"Now faith is the assurance of things hoped for, the conviction of things not seen."* Hebrews 11:1 The dictionary's definition of the word faith is, "complete trust or confidence in someone or something."

*When missionary John Paton was translating the Scripture for the South Sea islanders, he was unable to find a word in their vocabulary for the concept of believing, trusting, or having faith. He had no idea how he would convey that to them. One day while he was in his hut translating, a native came running up the stairs into Paton's study and flopped in a chair, exhausted. He said to Paton, *"It's so good to rest my whole weight in this chair."*

John Paton had his word: Faith is resting your whole weight on God. That word went into the translation of their New Testament and helped bring that civilization of natives to Christ. Believing is putting your whole weight on God. If God said it, then it's true, and we're to believe it.

**Read Romans 5:1-2**

> Faith in the redemptive work of Jesus on the cross gives us all we need. Does this scripture bring you peace? Are you really putting your whole weight on God? Why or Why not?

_____

_____

_____

_____

_____

_____

_____

_____

_____

_____

**Whispered Truth:** What current situation in your life is requiring you to lean on your faith more than ever before and not circumstances or your own strength? What can you do to focus on faith and not the situation? Maybe you need to journal or meditate on scripture to strengthen your faith. Maybe you need to remember the miracles and provision God has already given you and praise Him.

What truth is God whispering to you right now about faith? How will you apply the Word to your life?

___

*"And it is impossible to please God without faith. Anyone who wants to come to him must believe that God exists and that he rewards those who sincerely seek him."* Hebrews 11:6

*https://www.preceptaustin.org/romans_5-1-2

# *Whispered Truth*
# *Bible Study*
# *Lesson Three/Chap. 9-12*

## Truth

**Key Verse:**
*"Jesus said to the people who believed in him, 'You are truly my disciples if you remain faithful to my teachings. You will know the truth, and the truth will set you free."* John 8:31-32

God revealed the truth through Denise's friend. Betty, when she told her about the conversation, she overheard Doyle have with another employee. This gave Doyle the information he needed to frame the babysitter's husband. Then more truth is revealed to Denise, and Doyle's lie starts to unravel further when Jaime tells the therapist the 'secret' he has asked her to keep. Denise thinks knowing the truth about what is causing Jaime's behavior has got to be better than not knowing. Was knowing better than not knowing? The mortifying truth created rage and turmoil in Denise and flashbacks to her own abuse.

Is truth worth knowing and fighting for at all costs? Why do so many people live in denial rather than face the truth about devastating things in their lives?

_____
_____
_____
_____
_____
_____

**Read Matthew 10:26**

What does this verse say to us about truth and persecution?

_____
_____

Many people have 'secrets' in their families they have been told not to talk about or share with anyone. Families can be torn apart when members start to heal and talk about what went on in the family.

> Have you ever experienced this? Are family secrets ever worth keeping? Why or why not?

> How would you have responded to Jaime's secret? How would you have dealt with your anger? Would you have been mad at God or turned to Him grateful the truth came out? How would you use your faith in this situation?

**Read Ephesians 4:21 & John 16:13-14**

The truth comes from Jesus and His word. When Jesus left this world, He sent us the Holy Spirit and He guides us into all truth.

> Why does truth through the Holy Spirit bring glory to God? Tell of a time the Holy Spirit revealed truth to you that you needed to know to make a decision, have a better relationship or even to leave a relationship?

_____

_____

_____

_____

_____

_____

_____

_____

Personal change in our lives is not about having will power. It comes from knowing and facing the truth. You must be truthful with yourself about past events, relationships, finances, current circumstances, yourself—everything. This is so important because behind every self-defeating habit in your life is a lie that you believe. It's not always easy to face some truths, but the freedom you experience once you have allowed God shine His truth in your heart makes it worth it.

Are you absolutely certain that what you believe you've said is true? When you face the truth, you will see change in your life. Is the way you think about your past or about some event the truth, or is the truth what God says about it?

Spending daily quiet time in God's word and listening for His voice will bring truth. And change requires learning the truth.

> Spend some quiet time with the Lord and ask if there is anything in your life that you believe to be true that isn't—about your past or current situation or things you say about yourself. Write about it here.
>
> What does God say the truth is about what He has brought to your mind?

_____

_____

_____

_____

_____

_____

_____

_____

_____

**Whispered Truth:** What truth in your life has been covered up? How would things be different if you and others faced the truth of an impossible situation? Maybe you need to ask God to bring truth into that situation. Maybe you need to have a difficult conversation with someone in order to find healing.

What is God whispering to you right now? How will you apply this word to your life?

_____

_____

_____

_____

_____

_____

_____

_____

_____

_____

_____

_____

_____

_____

_____

_____

_____

> *"Instead, we will speak the truth in love, growing in every way more and more like Christ, who is the head of his body, the church."* Ephesians 4:15

# *Whispered Truth*
# *Bible Study*
# *Lesson Four/Chap. 13-16*

## Forgiveness

**Key Verse:** *"Get rid of all bitterness, rage and anger, brawling and slander, along with every form of malice. Be kind and compassionate to one another, forgiving each other, just as Christ has forgiven you."* Ephesians 4:31-32

Denise hears a tough sermon by Pastor Whit that challenges her belief system. She believes God could not possibly love Doyle because of his actions, then the sermon goes into forgiving the worst evil imaginable. Denise has a choice to make when the Holy Spirit wrestles with her heart later that day. God gives Denise a compassionate love for Doyle that wells up in her after she chooses to forgive. God's love is all encompassing, and His love breaks the bondage that the enemy creates when we choose unforgiveness. Forgiveness brings freedom from that bondage.

How does God help Denise make the choice to forgive Doyle and what insight does she gain?

_____
_____
_____
_____
_____

Have you ever visualized your enemy being harmed, like Denise's fantasy about Doyle being hit by a bus? If so, describe how you felt. How can this actually harm us and not our enemy?

_____
_____
_____
_____

### Read Isaiah 43:25-26

When Denise reads this scripture, she realizes that God wants to hear her feelings in that moment in her life. What does God say to you in this verse?

Does this encourage you? In what way(s)?

_____

_____

_____

_____

_____

_____

God's love and truth breaks Denise's anger and she chooses to forgive. Forgiveness is defined as "an **act of love, mercy, and grace**. Forgiveness is a decision to not hold something against another person, despite what they have done to you." In the Bible, the Greek word translated "forgiveness" literally means **"to let go,"** as when a person does not demand payment for a debt. Jesus used this comparison when he taught his followers to pray: "Forgive us our sins, for we ourselves also forgive everyone who is in debt to us."

### Read Luke 17:3-4 & John 20:21-23

According to these scriptures, what condition is required to forgive?

_____

_____

_____

Luke makes it clear that full forgiveness is only possible in response to true repentance. Trust and forgiveness are two very different things. If someone has abused you to get rid of the bitterness and anger, we need to ask God (it is a choice) to give us the supernatural ability to forgive. But God would never want us to forget that person's actions and trust them again, unless they had repented and received help to change. Even then, that individual must slowly earn our trust based on their future actions.

Forgiveness towards the unrepentant person is for us and heals our heart of the pain inflicted upon it. It is a choice and it is damaging if someone demands that we forgive before we have truly dealt with the sin done against us. The difference is that when a person who wronged us does not repent with confession and conversion (turning from sin to righteousness), he cuts off

*Whispered Truth – Bible Study*

the full work of forgiveness. We can still lay down our ill will and we can hand over our anger to God, but we cannot carry through with reconciliation or intimacy.

***Forgiveness of an unrepentant person doesn't look the same as forgiveness of a repentant person.***

>What does Denise fear will happen if she forgives Doyle? Is it necessary to tell someone you have forgiven them?
>
>___
>___
>___
>___
>___
>___
>___
>
>Tell of a time when you forgave an unrepentant person and a repentant person. What was the result?
>
>___
>___
>___
>___
>___
>___
>___

In **Romans 12:19** God tells us not to take revenge but to leave room for His wrath and He will repay. In **1 Peter 2:23** scripture tells us to hand it over to Him who judges justly again and again. Forgiveness is not about feeling good about horrible things.

**Read Matthew 18:6**

>What is the Holy Spirit personally saying to you in Matthew 18:6? Does this scripture bring you comfort? Why or Why not?
>
>___

**Whispered Truth:** What truth has God whispered to you about unforgiveness? What is God whispering to you right now? How will you apply what He has revealed to your life?

> "O Lord our God, you answered them; You were a forgiving God to them, and yet an avenger of their evil deeds"
> Psalm 99:8 NASB

# *Whispered Truth Bible Study Lesson Five/Chap. 17-20*

## Redemption

**Key Verse:**
*"And we know that God causes everything to work together for the good of those who love God and are called according to his purpose for them."* Romans 8:28

Denise is on the phone with a guy she went out with once. During this one-way conversation, she lifts up a prayer while he drones on and on about himself. In this prayer she asks God to help her find someone who would love her for who she is and not what they could get from her. Someone who would be her best friend and love her and the girls like they are his own. God answers that prayer by bringing Chris, an I.R.S. agent, back into her life when Doyle once again lies and cheats her out of money from her tax return. The Holy Spirit prompts her to make the call and that call gives Chris the courage he needs to ask Denise out. God uses **everything**, even someone else's lies to accomplish His will in our life.

How has God taken something bad in your life and turned it for good, answering prayer?

_____
_____
_____
_____
_____
_____

Give an example of a time when you chose to focus on the good God has worked out rather than the evil plan of the enemy that invaded your life through people?

_____
_____

_____

_____

_____

_____

_____

_____

**Read 1 Peter 2:6 & Luke 6:47-49**

What does 1 Peter 2:6 tell us happens when we make Christ our cornerstone?
What are the three main principles that build our spiritual house on solid rock in Luke 6:47-49?

_____

_____

_____

_____

What is a person like who builds his or her house on sand or the ground without a foundation?

_____

_____

_____

_____

Denise's life has started over with many blessings from God and her new family has built their life on Christ, the Cornerstone. But she is challenged when she is asked to explore the spiritual foundation her family of origin built when she was growing up. Was their house built on rock, the cornerstone of Jesus or quicksand that would sink them when the storms arrived? The storm from her past life hit her hard when the memories came flooding back from the deep dark abyss as Denise starts to write.

Describe what foundation, rock or sand, your parents created. How did this influence you then and how does it still impact you today?

_____

_____

*Whispered Truth – Bible Study*

Chris and Denise were building a strong foundation for their family. Do you think this helped Denise during her struggle with her past? Why or Why not?

## Read 1 Peter 2:9

Describe a time when God called you out of your darkness into His wonderful light. How were you able to show God's goodness to others?

**Whispered Truth:** Is your life built on Christ or do you sink in quicksand in the middle of the storms this life brings? What from your past needs light to shine on it to dispel darkness that holds you back from His purpose? Maybe you need to ask God to strengthen you to find healing from past lies you've told yourself.

What is God whispering to you right now? How will you apply this word to your life?

___

*"So humble yourselves before God. Resist the devil, and he will flee from you."*
James 4:7

# Whispered Truth
# Bible Study
# Lesson Six/Chap. 21-24

## Obedience

**Key Verse:**
*"We destroy every proud obstacle that keeps people from knowing God. We capture their rebellious thoughts and teach them to obey Christ."* 2 Corinthians 10:5

Denise is depressed and has been sleeping a lot, then starts to have panic attacks that only get worse after she receives a phone call from her father. The counselor encourages her to write about her abuse and she when she hears the words "*Go Write*", she finishes the letter and it helps her to start to heal. Denise is then confronted at church by Rose about being involved in the occult. Once again Denise is obedient and asks God to forgive her when she learns that visiting a psychic has opened a door to the enemy and creates fear that results in panic attacks.

Have you wanted to know the future so bad you visited a psychic or participated in other occultic practices? If so, how did that activity impact your life?

_____

_____

_____

_____

_____

_____

_____

_____

**Read Leviticus 20:6-8**

What does this scripture tell us about obedience and what we open ourselves up to when we disobey?

_____

_____

Tell of a time when you were in disobedience. What happened? What changed when you repented of your actions?

Denise's experience with the psychic and the prophetic through Don who prophesied to and her family, were very different. One experience caused fear the other brought hope and brought encouragement. Through Don's obedience, God miraculously healed Chris of debilitating depression. When God revealed the dangerous things Jaime was involved in, it was to stop the enemy's plans and give her understanding of the 'real side of evil' so God could delivery her. Jaime finally accepts Jesus after she realizes evil is real and all demonic activity stops in her room.

**Read Ephesians 6:12**

Tell of a time when you realized that there is a spiritual battle going on in this world for our souls and the souls of our loved ones. How have you taken your authority in Christ to win the battle?

### Read Matthew 12:43-45

Jesus is describing the spiritual condition of the generation. He warns that it is not enough to repent and remove sin but that continued obedience to His word is needed to fill the empty house or something worse can happen. When we come to Christ our 'home' is cleansed but we must continually fill our homes/hearts with Him.

### Read 2 Corinthians 12:20-21

The Corinthians experienced what happens when we are not intentional in our walk by keeping our home/heart filled with Christ.

    Explain a time you have had this experience or seen this happen to others?

_____

_____

_____

_____

_____

_____

_____

_____

_____

_____

During the period Jaime is experiencing demonic visitations in her room, Denise receives a powerful vision of Jesus' shed blood while praying. If you have never been cleansed by the blood of Christ, then may the scripture in 1 Peter 18-19 and the words spoken to Paul in Acts 22:16 at his conversion, move you to respond:

> ***"For you know that God paid a ransom to save you from the empty life you inherited from your ancestors. And it was not paid with mere gold or silver, which lose their value. It was the precious blood of Christ, the sinless, spotless Lamb of God."*** 1 Peter 1:18-19

***"What are you waiting for? Get up and be baptized. Have your sins washed away by calling on the name of the Lord."*** Acts 22:16

**Whispered Truth:** Do you need to be obedient to God's saving grace and respond to His whispered truth in your life? Maybe you need to ask Jesus into your heart. Maybe you need to recommit your heart and life to Him right now.

What is God whispering to you right now? How will you apply this word to your life?

_____

_____

_____

_____

_____

_____

_____

_____

_____

_____

_____

_____

_____

_____

_____

**"I have loved you even as the Father has loved me. Remain in my love."** John 15:9

# Whispered Truth
# Bible Study
# Lesson Seven/Chap. 25-29

## Trust

**Key Verse:**
*"Trust in the LORD with all your heart;
do not depend on your own understanding. Seek his will in all you do,
and he will show you which path to take."* Proverbs 3:5-6

Jaime has drawn a concerning picture in art class and gets angry and will not discuss it when Denise tries to talk to her. Then Jaime refuses to get surgery on her knee, hobbling all the way to her boyfriend's house after they get home from the hospital. During the All Saints Walk to raise money for Jaime's school, she is caught with LSD. Denise starts to realize all the times she had missed the signs that indicated Jaime was doing drugs. Jaime finally tells Denise the truth about what happened when she left the dance club, calling her in the middle of the night terrified. Jaime has been raped and Denise is overwhelmed with guilt. She blames herself that she couldn't protect her daughter from the dangerous decisions she has made. Drugs motivated all of Jaime's actions and resulted in serious consequences.

How far would you go to help someone you love? How would you ever trust that person again after you discovered everything had been a lie?

_____

_____

_____

_____

_____

It's hard to trust God in the moments when He is confirming an impossible choice that needs to be made. God confirms Chris and Denise's decision three times: they need to put Jaime in a long-term drug rehab. Denise is in emotional turmoil from the pain this decision will cause even though it's the tough love Jaime desperately needs.

Describe a time when you trusted an answer God gave, even though it created emotional pain.

_____

_____

_____

_____

_____

**Read Hebrews 12:11, Ephesians 6:4, & Proverbs 29:17**

The definition of discipline is: *"Training expected to produce a specific character or pattern of behavior, especially training that produces moral or mental improvement."*

There are consequences when we spoil the child and spare the rod. In **1 Samuel 2-4** Eli rebuked, his sons but did not relieve them of their duties as priests for the sin of treating the offering of the Lord with contempt and for having immoral affairs with women in the temple. Eli and his sons paid the ultimate price: they died because Eli would not discipline them to correct their behavior.

Jaime needed tough love—discipline—to keep her from continuing down a dangerous path of self-destruction. She needed to be honest with her family and God. No discipline is enjoyable, but we have all gone through these times that were necessary to redirect our actions and get us to a place of right living.

> Describe a time of 'tough love' or discipline of your child or discipline you received. Did you trust God through this challenging time? Why or why not? How did He refresh you and give you peace?

_____

_____

_____

_____

_____

_____

_____

_____

We can find a positive side to most situations in life. Jaime being in drug rehab gave the family peace from the drama her drug use caused and gave Denise a chance to focus on Samantha and Daniel.

> Tell of a time when positive things came out of a negative situation in your life.

___

### Read Ephesians 6: 10-12

Doyle got remarried without Jaime's knowledge and introduces Jaime to her new stepmother at a Teens Helping Teens family meeting. Jaime is furious she missed the wedding and takes her anger out on Denise by blaming her for the drug use and for putting her in the rehab.

> Have you ever been an easy target for someone else's fury when you did what was best for them and the enemy twisted their perspective? What does the above scripture reveal and how are we supposed to respond?

___

### Read Ephesians 6:13–18

When Jaime brings other girls' home from Teens Helping Teens to stay at night they are visited by evil spirits because of an open door into the demonic realm.

In your own words explain what the scripture above says we are to do in these situations. Tell of a time you put this scripture into practice or explain how Denise uses the principle from this scripture to rid the room of demonic spirits.

_____

_____

_____

_____

_____

_____

_____

**Whispered Truth:** Are you trusting God with all your heart (*thoughts, desires, passions, appetites, affections, purposes and endeavors) in every situation and seeking His whispered truth in your life? Maybe you need to turn over your will to Him. Maybe you need to be still and listen for His voice.

What is God whispering to you right now? How will you apply this word to your life?

_____

_____

_____

_____

_____

_____

_____

*John Maxwell's definition of heart. In Hebrew it means; It denotes a person's center for both physical and emotional-intellectual-moral activities; sometimes it is used figuratively for any inaccessible thing.*

***"Those who know your name trust in you,
for you, O LORD, do not abandon those who search for you."* Psalm 9:10**

# Whispered Truth
# Bible Study
# Lesson Eight/Chap. 30-32

## Perseverance

**Key Verse:**
*"Blessed is the one who perseveres under trial because, having stood the test, that person will receive the crown of life that the Lord has promised to those who love him."* **James 1:12**

Denise has persevered through so many trials and it was through experiencing God faithfulness in those trials that her faith has soared. Now she prays in tongues, a gift from God that helps her continue to persevere. God once again blesses Denise when He answers prayer and brings out the truth. Doyle writes a check to cover half the cost of drug rehab without even going in front of the judge when he is shown a letter from Jaime's psychologist. It stated that she was being treated for chemical dependency because of childhood incest. Denise rejoices that God gave her attorney the needed strategy that blesses them financial and forces Doyle to face some responsible for the harm he caused.

Write about a trial and *God's faithfulness in the middle* of it which helped you persevere and made your faith soar.

_____

_____

_____

_____

_____

**Read Romans 12: 9-12 & Colossians 1:11-12**

The definition of perseverance is, *"Continued effort to do or achieve something despite difficulties, failure, or opposition with activity being maintained in spite of these difficulties."*

There are times we all have felt like giving up, giving in or just stopping and turning around. Who can blame us? Life is extremely painful at times and rarely fair. But God gives us reassurance that He is with us and never leaves us through the trials. Then He gives us a shining example of perseverance—Jesus! He faced more opposition and pain in one short lifetime than most of us will ever face. We were saved through Jesus' perseverance!

> Write the key ideas from these verses that help you understand perseverance. Then describe what God wants to accomplish through your perseverance.

___

Denise will now have to lean on God as she perseveres through the biggest trial of her life—Jaime has run away. God asks Denise to *"let her go."* She visualizes laying Jaime on the altar and walks away. Now only God knows where she is and can protect her. During the next 3 weeks God is faithful and gives Denise the understanding she needs. Then He shows her where Jamie is in Florida. The word "**GO**" is strong and immediate as Holy Spirit impresses upon Denise that she must leave for Florida to find Jaime. Not having any other information, she is obedient and buys a one-way ticket to Pensacola. Ann lives an hour away by the airport; Denise asks to spend the night so she can get there by 5 am the next morning for the 6 am flight. Ann receives a call, right after Denise and Chris arrive, from a Pensacola Police Sergeant. He tells Denise that Jaime is in the Juvenile Detention Center and she will be release at 8am the next morning. She marvels at the miracle God has given them.

> Tell of a time when you had to blindly trust the voice of the Holy Spirit and felt like you were jumping off a cliff without a parachute?

___

Why did God reveal Denise's anger and release her from it on the plane? What was Denise filled with after this happened?

_____

_____

_____

_____

What did Denise have to continue to do before the Lord could help her? Psalm 37:5. Why was this so important?

_____

_____

What lies did the devil hiss into Denise's ear when she first saw Jaime and what triumphed or overcame the lies?

_____

_____

Give an example from your own life of what the enemy did to try to stop you from persevering.

_____

_____

_____

_____

_____

**Reread pages 288-290.** Tell of a time when words given by Holy Spirit, that might not have made sense, gave you the wisdom you needed to make the right choice and persevere.

_____

_____

_____

**Whispered Truth:** Are you triumphantly persevering through all the trials of this life full of peace and joy? Take the time to be still. Hold on to His *whispered truth* until it's all you trust and make it your most valued treasure for the journey ahead.

What is God whispering to you right now? How will you apply this word to your life?

***"We want each of you to show this same diligence to the very end, so that what you hope for may be fully realized."*** Hebrews 6:11

www.ingramcontent.com/pod-product-compliance
Lightning Source LLC
Chambersburg PA
CBHW081237080526
44587CB00022B/3980